Alphabet Trail

Mary Susan Carey

Hello big A and little a.
Where are you?
I see you, peek-a-boo.
It's fun to see you on the trail.
You like seeing me too, you say.
Hooray!

Hello big B and little b.
Where are you?
I see you, peek-a-boo.
It's fun to see you on the trail.
You like seeing me too, you say.
Hooray!

Hello big C and little c.
Where are you?
I see you, peek-a-boo.
It's fun to see you on the trail.
You like seeing me too, you say.
Hooray!

Hello big D and little d.
Where are you?
I see you, peek-a-boo.
It's fun to see you by the big rock.
You like seeing me too, you say.
Hooray!

Hello big F and little f.
Where are you?
I see you, peek-a-boo.
It's fun to see you beside the tree branch.
You like seeing me too, you say.
Hooray!

Hello big G and little g.
Where are you?
I see you, peek-a-boo.
It's fun to see you on your side.
You like seeing me too, you say.
Hooray!

Hello big H and little h.
Where are you?
I see you, peek-a-boo.
It's fun to see you under the branches.
You like seeing me too, you say.
Hooray!

Hello big I and little i.
Where are you?
I see you, peek-a-boo.
It's fun to see you on the tree's roots.
You like seeing me too, you say.
Hooray!

Hello big J and little j.
Where are you?
I see you, peek-a-boo.
It's fun to see you between two rocks.
You like seeing me too, you say.
Hooray!

Hello big K and little k.
Where are you?
I see you, peek-a-boo.
It's fun to see you on a shelf up the tree.
You like seeing me too, you say.
Hooray!

Hello big L and little l.
Where are you?
I see you, peek-a-boo.
It's fun to see you stuck in the leaves.
You like seeing me too, you say.
Hooray!

Hello big M and little m.
Where are you?
I see you, peek-a-boo.
It's fun to see you sitting near the bench.
You like seeing me too, you say.
Hooray!

Hello big N and little n.
Where are you?
I see you, peek-a-boo.
It's fun to see you at the foot of the bench.
You like seeing me too, you say.
Hooray!

Hello big O and little o.
Where are you?
I see you, peek-a-boo.
It's fun to see you on the fence rail.
You like seeing me too, you say.
Hooray!

Hello big P and little p.
Where are you?
I see you, peek-a-boo.
It's fun to see you beside the post.
You like seeing me too, you say.
Hooray!

Hello big happy face.
What happened to Q?
I don't see you. Boo-hoo.
It's still fun to see a big hello.
You like seeing me too, you say.
Hooray!

Hello big R and little r.
Where are you?
I see you, peek-a-boo.
It's fun to see you sitting on the fence.
You like seeing me too, you say.
Hooray!

Hello big S and little s.
Where are you?
I see you, peek-a-boo.
It's fun to see you hiding in the shade.
You like seeing me too, you say.
Hooray!

Hello big T and little t.
Where are you?
I see you, peek-a-boo.
It's fun to see you sitting next to a post.
You like seeing me too, you say.
Hooray!

Hello big U and little u.
Where are you?
I see you, peek-a-boo.
It's fun to see you on the boardwalk.
You like seeing me too, you say.
Hooray!

Hello big V and little v.
Where are you?
I see you, peek-a-boo.
It's fun to see you on the wooden fence rail.
You like seeing me too, you say.
Hooray!

Hello big W and little w.
Where are you?
I see you, peek-a-boo.
It's fun to see you at the bend in the fence.
You like seeing me too, you say.
Hooray!

Hello big X and little x.
Where are you?
I see you, peek-a-boo.
It's fun to see you leaning on the fence post.
You like seeing me too, you say.
Hooray!

Hello big Y and little y.
Where are you?
I see you, peek-a-boo.
It's fun to see you up on the fence post.
You like seeing me too, you say.
Hooray!

Hello big Z and little z.
Where are you?
I see you, peek-a-boo.
It's fun to see you at the end of the pathway.
You like seeing me too, you say.
Hooray!

It's the end of the trail and the alphabet too
This means goodbye, not hello to you.
Keep smiling and keep reading,
Whatever you do.
I had so much fun with the letters.
Hope you did too.

are   big   fun   like   I   it's   little

hello   me   on   say   see   sit

where   to   you

Sight Words to recognize on the Alphabet Trail

beside   by

between   bend

Spatial concept words

end   in   near   next

on   up   under

Contact Information

nurturedyoungins@gmail.com

Angeljournal.com

A Bit about Mary Susan Carey

I am a retired Primary School Specialist, Kindergarten, Elementary and Middle School teacher, Elementary School Consultant and Special Education Teacher. And I have taught hundreds of young children and supported them through their learning achievements. It is always a pleasure to guide and instruct children and I trust that this pleasure will also be your reward as you work with your child or the children in your care.

Much is changing in our world and we can barely grasp the meaning of it all. But as the tools, circumstances, expectations, opportunities and processes change, the need for literacy, thinking, self-directed problem solving, and the inner self confidence that comes from learning how, remains constant. In fact it is more necessary now than ever before. I too am a parent and grandmother. Parents are the most important teachers a child has. Your outlook becomes their attitude. Your living example affects who they aspire to become.

Thank you and have fun with your child as you support their learning and development.

Other Titles for Children
Mary Susan Carey

https://tinyurl.com/DoggyTimePrinting1-USA

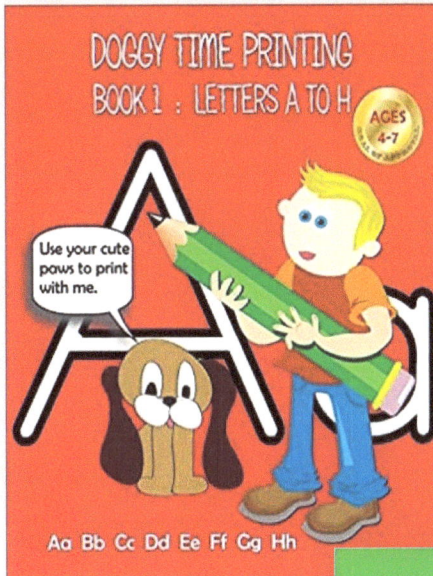

DOGGY TIME PRINTING
BOOK 1 : LETTERS A TO H
AGES 4-7

Use your cute paws to print with me.

Aa Bb Cc Dd Ee Ff Gg Hh

https://tinyurl.com
Magical-Unicorns-for-Girls-USA

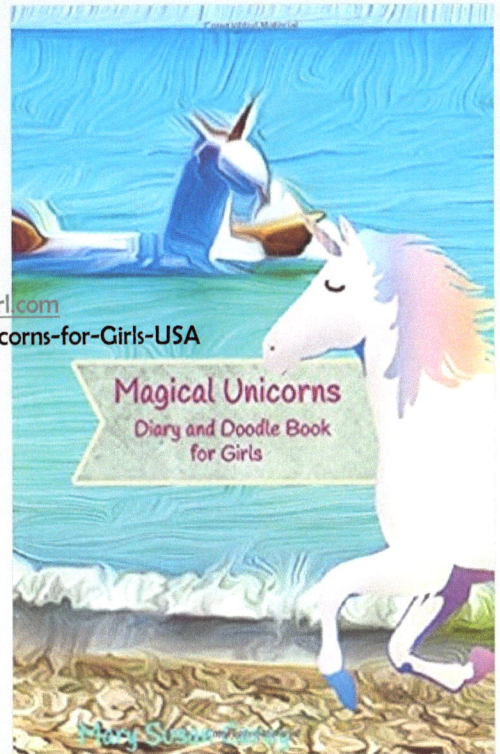

Magical Unicorns
Diary and Doodle Book
for Girls

Mary Susan Carey

Kindle Version
Alphabet Trail

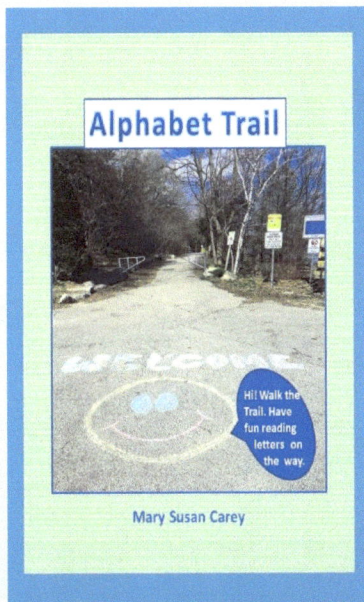

Alphabet Trail

Hi! Walk the Trail. Have fun reading letters on the way.

Mary Susan Carey

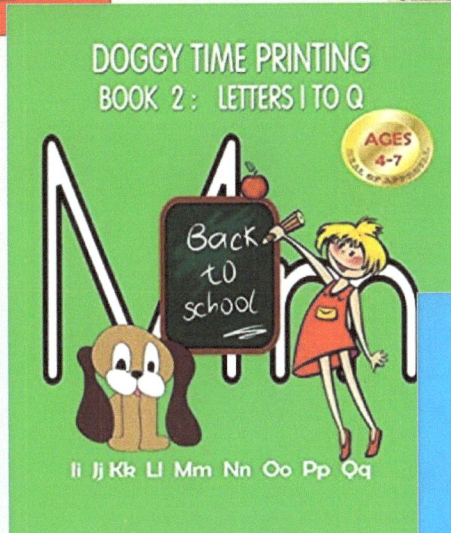

DOGGY TIME PRINTING
BOOK 2 : LETTERS I TO Q
AGES 4-7

Back to school

Ii Jj Kk Ll Mm Nn Oo Pp Qq

https://tinyurl.com/
DoggyTImePrinting2-USA

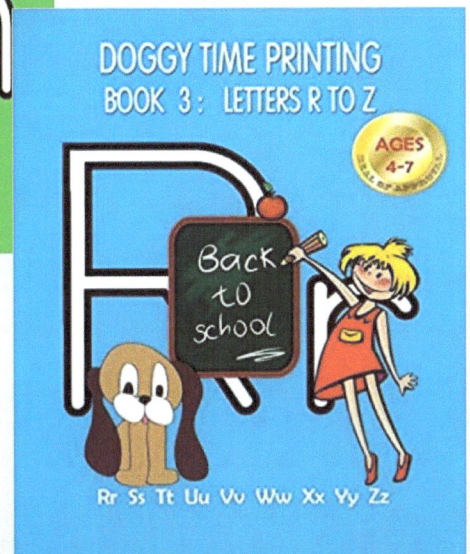

DOGGY TIME PRINTING
BOOK 3 : LETTERS R TO Z
AGES 4-7

Back to school

Rr Ss Tt Uu Vv Ww Xx Yy Zz

https://tinyurl.com
DoggyTimePrinting3-USA

Alphabet Trail

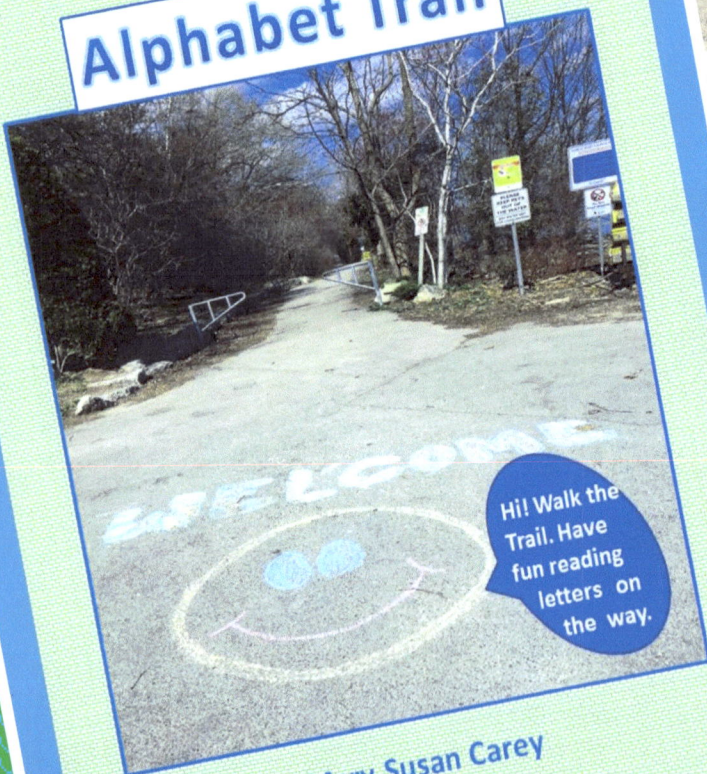

Hi! Walk the Trail. Have fun reading letters on the way.

Susan Carey

Alphabet Trail

Hi! Walk the Trail. Have fun reading letters on the way.

Mary Susan Carey

www.ingramcontent.com/pod-product-compliance
Lightning Source LLC
LaVergne TN
LVHW072118070426
835510LV00003B/118